THE ROSE
DRIFTING WITH DESTINY

玫瑰萍踪随缘漂流

Yao Lu

PREFACE

by Dr. Francesco Marincola

Inexorable, time passes. Sometimes it flows calmly down the watershed of life towards uncharted dark blue seas, other times it flies as an unreachable eagle. Little can be done to capture the moment as life freewheels around us like a whimsical butterfly. Yet, in rare circumstances, time solidifies into a vivid memory that sculpts the rest of one's life.

This is what I experience reading Yao Lu's poems; unforgettable vignettes of life painted with the magic of poetry.

前言

时光无情地流逝。有时它平静地从生活的分水岭流向未知的深蓝色海洋，其他时候它是一只遥不可及的鹰一样飞翔。当生活如同一只异想天开的蝴蝶在我们身边随心所欲地翩跹时，我们几乎无法捕捉到这一刻。然而，在极少数情况下，时间会定格成生动的记忆去塑造一个人的余生。

这就是我阅读姚露诗歌的感受：用诗歌的魔法描绘出令人难忘的生活片段。

WORD FROM THE AUTHOR

Man is a social being, and each person is inevitably labeled in society in many ways. These labels are fixed impressions formed in the group's subconscious through a combination of elements such as a person's profession, personality, and interests. As a young girl, I was obsessed with spending my days alone in a closed room, reading all sorts of famous novels and aspiring to become a professional writer. But my childhood dream was far from the label real life had given me, and it was like a crystal ball locked away in the dusty halls of memory.

It was only after the outbreak of the coronavirus that I began to write professionally, and the travel ban and strict quarantine made me look out of the window for a long time and do nothing but reading and writing poetry, as all true poets do, to express my innermost pain.

I read the works of great Western poets such as Whitman, Yeats and Wordsworth, while reciting many famous ancient Chinese texts, Tang poems, and song lyrics by heart during my nine years of compulsory education. Emily Dickinson said of the literary genre of poetry, "What a frugal vehicle it is for conveying the soul of man, that this channel can be trodden by the poorest of men and need not hurt." Walt Whitman introduced himself in a way that elicited a soft laugh from me, "A cosmic son of Manhattan, restless, fat, horny, eating, drinking, reproducing ...". I admire the complex emotional life of William Butler Yeats: "I see the fingers of the wind intimate, the delicate gestures shattered, I see the petals blown away in droves, O rose, poor lovesick rose!"

I read poetry but never learned to write it, so readers may find errors in the texts and techniques herein. This is my kind of poetry — a fusion of traditional ancient Chinese poetry, modern Western poetic forms, and a sense of real events. In my writings, I have also tried to explore and integrate Greek mythology, Chinese folktales, love and affection, and many other themes.

This book was fortunate to be accepted by a professional publisher, and on the occasion of the publication of this collection of poems, I forgot for a while the mud of my feet in the commercial world and immersed myself in something that really gives me a spark of inspiration.

Through my writings, it is my desire to share the ecology of different industries, the humanities of different countries, and different perspectives with readers around the world through the language of poetry. More importantly, it is my hope that all those who have contributed to the publication of this book accept and appreciate the criticism of our readers without bias so that we can continue on the path of discovering the value of creativity and imagination.

致读者们

　　人类是社会性动物，每个人在社会中一定会被贴上许多标签，这些标签是群体潜意识里通过个体职业、性格和兴趣等要素综合分析形成的固化印象。当我还是个不谙世故的小女孩时，我便痴迷于成天独自待在封闭的房间里阅读各种名著小说，渴望成为一名职业作家。只不过孩童时代的梦想离现实生活赋予我的标签很遥远，它像是最喜爱的那颗水晶球封存在蒙尘的记忆殿堂中。

　　直到新型冠状病毒爆发以后我才开始尝试职业写作，旅行禁令和严格的隔离措施让我在很长一段时间内选择透过窗户看外面的风景，闲来无事只能阅读和写诗，如同所有真正的诗人们一样，用诗歌抒发内心的极度苦闷。我读惠特曼、叶芝和华兹华斯等西方大诗人的作品，同时九年义务教育让我能熟练背诵不少中国古代名家文章和唐诗宋词。正如艾米莉·狄金森评价诗歌这种文学体裁："这渠道最穷的人也能走，不必为通行税伤神，这是何等节俭的车，承载着人的灵魂。"沃尔特·惠特曼自我介绍时让我发出轻笑，"一个宇宙，曼哈顿的儿子，躁动，肥壮，好色，吃着，喝着，生殖着……"我欣赏威廉·巴特勒·叶芝复杂的感情生活，"我看见风的手指狎昵，那横遭摧残的娇艳姿色，我看见花瓣被纷纷吹落，玫瑰啊，可怜害相思的玫瑰！"我读诗但从来没有学习过写诗，因此读者们会发现语法和技巧的诸多瑕疵。与其说我写的是诗歌，不如说这只是中国传统古诗词、西方现代诗歌形式和真实事件感悟融合的产物。我一直尝试去探索希腊神话、中国民间故事、爱情和亲情等更多主题。

　　本书有幸得到专业出版社的认可，值此诗集发行之际，我暂时忘记了脚踏在商业社会中的泥泞，潜心投入到真正能赋予自己灵感火花的事情中。我希望以微薄之力，通过诗歌这种语言向全世界的读者们分享不同行业的生态、不同国家的人文风情和不同角度的认知。更重要的是，作者和所有为本书出版工作做出贡献的人们将以开放的心态接受和感激读者们的批评指正，以便我们在发现创造力和想象力的价值这条路上能够走的更远。

COPYRIGHT

Copyright © 2022 by Yao Lu and MeiGuiLu Publishing.

All rights reserved. This book or any portion thereof may not be reproduced or used in any manner whatsoever without the express written permission of the publisher and the author except for the use of brief quotations in a book review.

Printed in the United Kingdom.

First Printing, 2022

TABLE OF CONTENT

11	The Kite
13	In My Life
15	The Full Moon
17	The Flight Record
19	I Have Disappeared
21	I'm Not in Your Garden
23	One Day
25	Grappling with Life
27	The Unreachable Star
29	I Came into this World
31	The Seed
33	The Unchanged Love
35	An Ode to the West Lake
37	A Long and Rough Journey
39	A Letter Home
41	The Adventures of the Rose

TABLE OF CONTENT

43	Don't Wake Me Up
45	Freedom
47	The Rebirth of a Poem
49	Deep at Night
51	The Moon Rises Again
53	Fragments
55	Nightmare
57	Bring me a Rose
59	The Relationship
61	An Ode to the Motherland
63	The Meaning of Existence
65	The Russian Dolls of Sappho
67	Souls
69	The Cat Behind the Window
71	Wind Chimes
73	The Echoes of Melody at Night

风筝

我轻掩门扉,
从逐渐变窄的门缝中瞅见,
母亲站在家门口假意目送我离开。
我心知我没有办法远走高飞
去自由探索天空的湛蓝,
我被一根透明的牢固的线系着,
这一次也不例外,
那个两鬓如霜的女人,
嘴巴祝我一路顺风的同时,
双手紧紧握着线轮。

The Kite

I gently pulled the door close,
glancing through the narrowing crack.
In the courtyard, mother insincerely bade me a farewell.
I knew in my heart I couldn't go far
to fly freely into the blue sky,
as I was bound to a thread invisible but strong.
And this time is not an exception.
The woman with grey temples,
she wished me a pleasant journey,
but the reel in her hands she held all the more tightly.

我这一生

我这一生，青春溘然长逝。
我是一株散尽幽香的兰花暗自凋零。

我这一生，时间转瞬即逝。
我是一颗纵情燃烧的彗星快速坠地。

我这一生，
我没有读懂其他人，其他人也不能读懂我。
我不是钩章棘句，却长久地束之高阁。

我这一生，
我无法靠近任何人，任何人也不能靠近我。
我不是阳春白雪，却融化地无声无息。

在我的一生中，
仍然感激被翻阅，
仍然期待被倾听。

In My Life

In my life, youth relentlessly faded.
I am but a withering orchid with fragrance long gone.

In my life, time swiftly passed.
I am a burning comet fast plummeting to the ground.

In my life,
I cannot peer into the thoughts of others, nor can they into mine.
I am not difficult to read, but I gathered only dust on a lonely shelf.

In my life,
I cannot get into anyone's heart, but neither can they into mine.
I am not like the snow at the dawn of Spring, but I silently melt.

In my life,
I am still grateful to be read,
and I am still eager to be heard.

满月

家中的盆栽遵循季节规律黄了树叶，
一阵午后的秋雨浇开了院里的红花。

自从白玉盘挂在漆黑的帷幕之上，
百褶窗前离开的信鸽便渺无音讯。

皎洁的月色一如既往笼罩着神州大地，
亘古不变，你我好比东流水。

周遭寂静，
只是此心还是像水中的月亮波光荡漾，
破碎，虚晃，有声响。
何曾有人去拯救那道光芒？

The Full Moon

The leaves of the bonsai trees at home grew yellow
as a season gave way to another.
The red flowers in the courtyard bloom
after an autumn afternoon rain.

From the moment the moon hung amidst the tenebrous velvet sky,
the pigeons departed the window shutters,
and are now lost in sight.

The bright moon shines upon the earth as it always does.

You and I are like rivers that flow east,
as they always have.

Silence reigns.

But the heart is still like the moon
on the rippling and glistening water,

broken, flickering, and sighing.

But alas, tell me…
did we at all strive
to keep that moon shining in our hearts?

飞行记录

万丈霞光刺破流云,
惊扰了坐在窗边睡眼惺忪的旅人。
天空抛却肃穆庄重,
轻佻地揭开了大地的面纱。
钢筋水泥丛林中,几座山丘露出绿色额头,
匆忙的巨轮驶过蓝色水面,藏不住身后的白色长尾巴。
疲倦的飞鸟终有落地时——
尽管它仍在空中,
艳羡着一艘悠哉的渔船停泊在那码头。

The Flight Record

The radiant glow pierces the drifting clouds of crimson,
distracting the sleepy travelers sitting by the window.
The sky has abandoned its solemnity,
unraveling the Earth's wondrous dawn.

In the concrete jungle below,
several hills raise their green foreheads.
A giant ship sails hastily across the blue water,
unable to conceal its long white trail behind.
And the tired bird would sooner or later land —
but for now, it flies high above the sky,
admiring a boat moored at the pier, leisurely fishing.

消失

我已消失,永远地。
我不知道我为什么永远地消失了,
他们说一场疾病带走了我。

在消失之前,
我的多动症痊愈了,
我开着汽车与不醒目的路边树亲密接触,
我迈着失败的步伐进行了一场成功的骨科手术,
我忘记一个老朋友的姓名,
我偶尔回想起年少时的恋人,
如今,
我接受自己是个平凡的大人。
在我消失之前,
我的头发在消失,
老友的头发也在消失。

邪恶势力在攻击我,
谁丢下了自保武器和防御铠甲?
总之我已消失……
如同一盏熄灭的灯。

重新点亮我!
将我挂在大世界的夜空中,
长明如星光,

凝望着你慢慢忘记我…

I Have Disappeared

I have disappeared forever.
I don't know why.
They say a disease took my life.

Before I disappeared,
my ADHD was seemingly cured.
Before I disappeared, I drove the car in intimate contact
with the mundane roadside trees.
Before I disappeared, I shuffled
and went through a successful orthopedic operation.
Before I disappeared,
I failed to remember the name of an old friend…
but I occasionally thought of my young lover.

Before I disappeared,
I have accepted that
I was but an ordinary adult.
I started losing my hair,
and so did my old friend.

Unseen and malevolent forces struck me,
and forsaking my arms and armor, I have disappeared.
Yes, I have disappeared…
like a quenched lamp I vanished.

Oh, rekindle me, rekindle me,
and cast me in the vastness of the night sky.
There, I will shine like the brilliant stars,
and gaze at you gradually forgetting me.

我不在你的花园里

懒惰的园丁,湿冷的空气来袭,
请像保护蔬菜那样,用温暖的稻草盖住我,
使我不畏惧白雪堆积。

下雪的日子万籁俱寂,
这令我有些想念春雨细密,
和夏日茂盛树叶缝隙中漏出的光影。
更多的时候,我会想念
人类庆祝果实和它们母亲的分离。

雪花铺满了花园里唯一的路径,
我该提醒你将屋内的炉火燃起,
再披上散发着樟脑丸香气的棉衣。

懒惰的园丁,我并没有扎根在你的花园里,
直到金色的眉毛染上惆怅的白,
这里还是荒草丛生,无人打理。
我想,我可以移植到别处,土壤更肥沃的方寸之地,

总有好心人来将我灌溉,信或不信,
明天,我便不在你的花园里。

I'm Not in Your Garden

Lazy gardener, the moist and chilly wind is blowing.
Please cover me with warm straw
like how you protect the vegetables,
dispelling my fear of the heavy snow.

Stillness reigns on this snowy day,
leaving me yearning for springtime rain,
I'm longing to see the play of light
and shadow of the lush trees of summer,
Oh, how much I will miss the celebration
for the parting of fruits from their mother.

Snow has draped the only path in the garden.
I ought to remind you to light the fire in the fireplace,
and put on a cotton coat with the whiff of mothballs.

Lazy gardener, I did not take root in your garden.
Till the golden leaves fade in gloom on a bed of white snow;
unattended, your garden shall see weeds irrepressibly grow.

Oh, I could have been transplanted somewhere else —
perhaps in fertile land.

Oh, there will always be kind people
who could come and water me,
But from tomorrow on, lazy gardener,
in your garden, I shall no longer be.

一天

你的模样我早已忘记,
可每年这天我又忆起。

那天无风逐浪,人海静谧,
轻飘飘的小舟泛于心湖上。

那天装饰城市的彩灯亮起,
纷纷扬扬的白星星,
有些落在你的肩头上,
还有一些落在你影子的肩头上。

有路人察觉到
那天尘世中一颗没有变成珍珠的沙砾
偶然地住进了我的眼中吗?

今天春风催促新芽,
你曾妄断,
那沉寂许久的枯木不会再萌动,
你且耐心等待,再等待一会吧,
最多再等待几分钟,
情愫是地下河在流淌,地上树迎风又长。

One Day

I have forgotten what you look like.
But on this day every year, I remember it all over again.

The crowd was quiet.
With no wind hounding the waves at that time,
a light boat floats on the serene lake of heart.

The colorful lanterns that adorned the city lit up that day,
twinkling like a myriad of white stars,
with some falling on your shoulders,
and others, on that of your shadow.

Were there any passers-by that day
that noticed that among the countless grains of sand,
an ordinary grain has unknowingly caught my sight
and turned into a pearl before my eyes?

Today, the gentle breeze of Spring awakens new buds.
You once curtly claimed that
the slumbering and seemingly lifeless woods
would never again spring to life.
But be patient! Wait a little longer —
it will take just a few minutes more.
For the most intimate feelings are the flowing underground rivers,
that nurture the trees on the ground, rising against the wind.

与生活竞技

拆开绷带吧!
流血的伤口已经愈合。
生活是我的敌人,
我执意在堡垒里与它作战后留下了勋章。

不要召唤我!
枪膛的子弹快要耗尽。
生活不是我的敌人,
我放弃在堡垒里与它作战后扬起了白旗。

我收到一封信:
亲爱的John,
你打算什么时候结束战斗?

我也在等待浓雾硝烟散去,
让破旧的牛仔帽躺在角落。
我试图在羊皮纸上写下真实想法,
提起半截炭笔的手却如此无力。

打开牢笼吧!
生活与我在同一个竞技场。
就当我弃甲投戈,
旁观者知道没有人是胜者;
当我落荒而逃时,
我们都知道没有人是胜者。

Grappling with Life

Take off the bandage!
For the bleeding wound has healed.
Life has been my foe,
and medals hung in the fort after fighting against it.

Don't beckon me back!
The bullets in the barrel are about to run out.
Life is not my enemy.
I gave up the fight and flew the white flag in the fort.

I received a letter:
Dear John,
when will you return from the battlefield?

I'm also waiting for the heavy fog and thick smoke to clear.
Let the shabby cowboy hat lie in the corner.
I have tried to write down my thoughts on a parchment,
but my hand is too weak to lift the pen.

Open the cage!
Life stares me down in the same arena.
As I see no other choice but to give up the fight,
the spectators see no winner.
And when I have eluded and have gone,
then we shall all come to understand
that in the arena of life,
no one ever emerges victorious.

遥不可及

夜沉如水,
新的一年人们许下各自的愿望,
像是阳台上的风铃在轻诉着,
我无从得知。

朋友,愿你健康喜乐。
健康绝非易事,
快乐更是奢侈。
还有……
愿望竟多如繁星,
高悬在天空上不可能拥有,
我画了一架云梯,
穷途跋涉,
只为能摘下属于自己的那颗。
从今以后,
愿我对幸福敏感,对悲伤迟钝。

若它遥不可及,
那就让我站在银河河带上,
倾听群星讲述古老的传说。

The Unreachable Star

The night is long like waters run deep.
Each soul whispers their wishes for the New Year,
like wind chimes tinkling on the balcony.
I have no way of knowing what they have wished for.

But my friends, may you be healthy and happy.
To be healthy is a struggle,
and to find happiness is rather a luxury.

And you know...
The multitude of wishes are like the endless scattered stars,
sparkling high in the sky beyond anyone's grasp.
I drew a ladder to reach for the clouds.
And going through a long and assiduous journey,
I want to reach for the one that belongs to me.

And from now on,
I wish myself nothing but happiness,
and may there be no more room for sadness.

And if it is truly unreachable,
let me then stand on the river belt of the Milky Way,
that I may listen to the stars narrate their stories of old.

我来到这世上

我十万次问:
我来到这世上的准确时辰。

只能得到一份模糊的答案。

我第一次成为我,
母亲第一次成为母亲,
父亲第一次成为父亲。
我的小船将要在人生大海上航行,
只能靠这两个没有经验的新舵手。

母亲再三叮嘱父亲戴上新买的手表。
为什么我十万次问
只能得到一份模糊的答案?

父亲漫不经心地站在空荡的楼道里发呆。

兴许灰白墙上的挂钟能回答
我来到这世上的准确时辰。

嘀嗒嘀嗒……
斜阳随着指针悠悠绕过山岗,
月亮接替它的工作给了我光,
与此同时每个人打开了家中的电灯,
我来到这世上。

I Came into this World

I asked time and time again
for the precise moment I came into this world.
But I have only received vague answers.

I opened my eyes to the world.
Mom became a mother for the first time.
So did Dad.
My tiny and fragile boat would soon sail on the vast ocean of life,
steered by these two inexperienced sailors.

Mom kept telling Dad to wear his newly bought watch
so that he would know
the answer to the question I have been asking since then…
And alas, I received a vague response once again.
Father simply stood in the empty corridor without a tinge of
expression.

But perhaps the clock on the gray wall could tell me now
the precise moment I came into this world somehow.

Tick-tock, tick-tock
The sun sets gently, bidding the hills farewell with each tick.
Taking over, the moon softly graces the horizon
and casts its subtle light.
And as lamps were lit in homes in the stillness of the night,
I came to this world and opened my eyes to its sight.

种子

看看一粒种子沉眠进黑土地中
能够长出怎样的植物来？

它大概率是——
一朵娇艳明丽的花；
一棵苍翠挺拔的树。
不管它是——
一朵弱不禁风的花；
一棵根深叶茂的树。
不管它是——
怡然自得——
奋力向上——
它都会
以花瓣或落叶的形式
重返回黑土地中。
像——
一根头发脱落；
一个细胞凋亡。

看看一粒种子沉眠进黑土地中
能够长出怎样的植物来？
这次同眠的还有一只掉队的羚羊。

The Seed

A humble seed lay dormant underneath the black soil...
what kind of plant will it grow into?

Perhaps it shall sprout into
a delicate and beautiful flower,
or a perhaps lush and upright tree.

No matter what it may be, be it a delicate blossom
or a tree, deeply rooted and embellished with virescent leaves,
be it happy and content with ease
or struggling to break out and proudly rise,
alas, it shall return to the embrace of the black soil
in the form of faded petals and fallen leaves,
like hair falling out or a dying cell.

A humble seed lay dormant underneath the black soil...
what kind of plant can it grow into?
But forget not that this very black soil
is also the final resting place
of an antelope that once lagged behind its flock.

永恒的爱

当我们沉默告别,
可能预料今生再无缘相见?
最后一次温柔注视,我的爱人。

我还能爱你多久?
我爱你像绵延不绝的山脉跨越人为的边界;
我爱你像一朵生生不息的太阳花,
风中用厚实双手护住的熊熊火焰;
我爱你是仲夏夜晚里无法噤声的聒噪蝉鸣;
我爱你的回声离开幽静的山谷传到目光不及之处。
至此我爱你的心事无需宣扬,
它作为既定事实写在我眼角和嘴角的纹路里,
藏在双唇轻启发出的尾音中——
我主动发誓,即使在那之后,
我爱你的感觉还是如同钻石般永远纯粹!

The Unchanged Love

When we bid each other farewell in silence,
Did we suppose that we would never see each other again
in this lifetime?
Cast upon me your tender gaze for the last time, my love.

How long shall I lay this love upon you?
It is like an endless mountain range across man-made borders,
like a blossoming sunflower,
and a dancing flame cupped by sturdy hands in the wind.
It is like the cicadas that cannot be silenced
on the midsummer night;
and its echo rings through the idyllic valley
to where our eyes cannot reach.

In the depths of my heart, it need not be uttered.
It has crept into the folds of my eyes and mouth,
hidden in the intricate sound
uttered through my gently opened lips.

And to you, I pledge, even after this farewell,
that the love in my heart, which is still like a diamond,
will always remain pure and crystal clear.

西湖颂

西湖水流千载,
数不尽的文人骚客留下墨宝把它唱,
多一个人来画蛇添足又何妨?

西湖水流千载,
雨中湖面飘摇的渡船还渡有缘人啊……
断桥上停留的人转过身来吧!
记得将借来的油纸伞还予他。

这大好的湖光山色,
风晴雨雪天,
他来看过吗?
恰好与她踏过了西湖边上的同一块石板吗?
在青芝坞露台上听雨到天明的人等你应答……

An Ode to the West Lake

The West Lake has endured for thousands of years.
Already countless writers and poets have left verses and odes,
so would it matter if there is still one more?

The West Lake has endured for thousands of years.
The boat bobbing on the rain-splashed lake
carries my destined better half.
Oh, you waiting on the Broken Bridge, do turn around,
and remember to give him back the paper umbrella he lent you.

This great scale of lakes and hills
emerges on a bright sunny day,
after the wind blows the rain or snow away.
Has he ever visited this picturesque place…
he who stepped by chance
on the same slab of stone by the lake as she?
And she who listened to the nightly rain
until the first light of dawn,
remaining still on the open terrace of Qingzhiwu,
yes, she — she is still waiting for an answer.

迷途

黄沙漫天我徒步行走在大漠上,
马匹在去往绿洲的半道上死亡,
乌云蔽日前路渺茫。
在陌生旅客们生起的一堆篝火旁,
巨婴蜷缩成一团
回到最初的梦乡,
温暖的子宫里
感受不到世态炎凉,
睡脸上诠释着难以掩饰的心伤,
醒来拭去泪水再次背起行囊,
天亮继续前往未知远方。

A Long and Rough Journey

As I crossed the desert, a yellow sandstorm blew.
The horse perished on the way to the oasis.
Dark clouds engulfed the long road ahead.
Next to a campfire lit by wayfarers,
a giant baby curled up and fell asleep.

His dream brought him back
to the bliss he once knew in his mother's warm womb,
where the fickleness of the world was kept at bay.

Unshrouded sorrow crept over his listless and sleepy face.
And wiping his tears after his waking,
with his knapsack on his back,
he marched on at the sight of dawn,
he marched on into the horizon unknown.

一封家书

妈妈，在迷宫里我走了很长一段路，分不清东南西北，可我的双脚还踏在干净的泥块上，罪恶之花无法生长。

妈妈，举起你手中的那盏煤油灯，那道光，宛如黑夜大海上闪烁着的灯塔，微弱，足够明亮，为我指示正确方向。

妈妈，我听说姐姐的第二个小孩已经出生。战火纷飞的年代，死亡的阴霾挥之不去，与之并存的是新生的希望。

妈妈，我凝视深渊的瞬间，只是一场梦魇。在和煦的微风里，人们结伴出游，笑语晏晏，你也随他们一起去踏青吧，共赏春日河堤桃花，切勿辜负明媚春光。

（你询问我的近况？）

我虽擅长舞文弄墨，这次却言辞匮乏，不知如何描述在这条人迹罕至的路上见到的风景：玻璃杯盛满清水，一颗掉进水里的药丸，失去糖衣的包裹，入口全是苦涩，用来治疗高血压。

我走了很长一段路，时间久到电影票上的字褪色了。我们是路上成群结队的牛羊，一整天在山坡上吃草，摇摇尾巴，尽兴晚归。跟紧庞大的队伍，多一只，少一只，审计出错很正常。

妈妈，我拿童年时期在储蓄罐里积攒的所有快乐硬币去交换成年人在冷酷世界的一次大口喘气。再见时，
我恐怕不再是少年模样。

A Letter Home

Mom, I have gone a long way through the labyrinth without finding a way out. But my feet are still rooted in the clean mud, warding off the wiles of venomous flowers.

Mom, please lift the kerosene lamp in your hand. The light, dim as it may be, is like a flickering beacon on the night sea, bright enough to guide me to your safe harbor.

Mom, I heard that my sister gave birth to her second child.
War-torn times are cloaked in the lingering breath of death, but there is yet a spark of hope.

The moment I stare into the abyss is but a nightmare. But amidst the gentle breeze, people go out in twos and threes, talking and laughing. Please go out with them and greet the freshness of spring outside. Delight in the peach blossoms on the riverside and never miss the lively and beautiful spring.

(And since you asked how I've been doing:)

As good as I am at writing, I am at a loss for words.

I don't know how to express the scenes along the paths untrodden: a full glass of water, a pill that has fallen in, its sugar coating lost, and the bitter taste that fills my mouth, all to relieve hypertension.

I have journeyed a long way — that far that the words on the movie tickets have faded. We are a herd of cattle and sheep on the road. After grazing all day on the hills, we come home late, with tails wagging. Striving to keep up with the huge herd, one more or maybe one less, both are the usual mistakes in counting.

Mom, I spent all the happy coins from my childhood piggy bank to breathe a sigh of relief in this cold world of grown-ups. And when we meet again, I fear I will no longer be the young child you remember.

玫瑰的冒险

一朵极其普通的玫瑰正在旅行……
天气总是瞬息万变,
暴风雪欲将她埋掩,
骄阳似火灼烧胸膛,
岁月寒来暑往。

她途经一条河,和叶子们漂浮在水面,调皮的水草戏弄她,
她途经一座山,空气从温暖变得寒冷,再从寒冷变得温暖,

大好河山试图挽留她,但……
她不是一条在淡水里生活的鲤鱼,
亦不是一棵生长在亚寒带的云杉,

她只是一朵极其普通的玫瑰,
渴望绽放成一朵耀眼的烟花。

"有人在那里吗?任何人?"
玫瑰向林中女巫们发问。

一只好心的夜莺告诉她,
"村庄爆发了一场大瘟疫,
当房屋是坚固的牢笼,
人们便是乖巧的囚犯。
我在枝头停止了歌唱,
歌声无法治愈那悲怆。"

玫瑰闻言倒在大片柔软的青草地上,
为人间悲剧献上了自己无声的挽歌。

The Adventures of the Rose

An ordinary rose is on her journey...
the weather keeps changing abruptly.
A snowstorm comes to engulf her.
The scorching sun burns her dainty skin.
Winter is over, and spring and summer are around the corner.

She crosses a river,
she flows on the water, swamped with impertinent weeds;
she climbs a mountain,
and is greeted by snug warmth that quickly gave way
to the icy breath of cold,
and then from frigidity back to the fervor of heat.

The beauteous terrain stalls her steps,
but she is not a carp swimming in fresh water,
nor is she spruce that grows in the subfrigid tundra.

She is but an ordinary rose,
longing to bloom like a brilliant firework.

"Is there anyone out there? Hello?"
She asked the witches of the forest.
A kind-hearted nightingale told her,
"A great plague broke out in the village.
The houses have turned into concrete cages,
and people inside had become helpless prisoners.
I stopped singing atop the trees,
for it can no longer dispel their griefs."

At these words, the rose collapsed in weary on the soft grassy field,
and devoted her silent elegy to the tragedy of the world revealed.

别唤醒我

别唤醒我！
我从未正视镜中之人，
自命不凡的我
在左胸膛里佩戴着一颗自恋的心灵。
让我不知道
我不知道的事实
沉入大海。
我笃定自己被豢养的猪猡更高贵！

Don't Wake Me Up

Don't wake me up!
Complacent and conceited,
I never contemplate myself in the mirror.

Pretentious, I harbor a narcissistic heart in my left chest,
and how it blinds me
to the truth that I should have faced —
to the truth that I can't help but sink into a fathomless sea.

Yet my faith keeps convincing me
that I am much nobler than even a noble pig.

诗人谈自由

人们试图寻找我 ——
那时的我已经难觅踪迹。
我隐匿在白云深处，躲藏在巍峨青山的另一侧。
缤纷的红叶将我的足迹埋没，
经验丰富的猎人对此束手无策。

你们最好忘记
我的名字，相貌，声音——
一切微不足道的信息。
我抛弃了肩膀上的所有责任，
你们尽管嘲笑我的懦夫行径，
分贝再大都无法传到我耳中。

我祝福每一个好的灵魂被幸运女神眷顾，
获得的喜悦感染了周围所有人，
除此之外，我不能做更多，
我也不会参与到那欢乐的气氛中。

在漫漫岁月里我一路撒下诗歌的星火……
除此之外，我离开时没有留下任何明显的线索。

Freedom

How many times have they tried to look for me —
it is not easy to find a trace of who I used to be.
I hid on the other side of the towering green mountain,
shrouded in thick white clouds.
The colored autumn leaves have buried my footprints,
bewildering even a seasoned hunter.

So, you're better off forgetting
my name, my face, and my voice —
all these are now but trivial information.

I shrug off all the duties that have fallen on my shoulders.
Yes, you may laugh at my cowardice,
in fact, laugh as loud as you can...
for it will only fall on deaf ears.

May every good soul be favored by the Goddess of Luck.
Your joy is contagious.
but all I can do is wish you luck,
for I chose to seclude myself from this joyous atmosphere.

For years, I have strewn poetic embers along the path I trod.
But I left no trace of those when I departed.

诗

诗人——
有时候会担心诗歌的泉眼干涸，
灵感不再从大脑的山涧流过。

智者说不必多虑，
年轻的泉眼，
你看——
休眠百年的火山会喷发，
只要痛苦——
开始在心里翻江倒海。

闸口打开，
岩浆得以宣泄而出。

短暂的愉悦——
要花很多时间怅惘，
将一缕缕愁思编织成厚密的
名为想象力的翅膀，
新诗在灰烬中涅槃重生。
飞翔……

The Rebirth of a Poem

As a poet,
she sometimes worries that the wellspring of poetry will dry up,
and that inspiration will cease to flow from the depths of the mind.

Then a wise man told her not to worry too much.
Young poet, you see...
A volcano that has been dormant for a hundred years
will again erupt,
once the pain starts to overwhelm its heart.
With its mouth open,
magma will be spewed out.

The short-lived joy left the poet plentiful time to be melancholic.
It weaved wisps of feeling
into full-fledged wings called the *imagination*.
And behold — a new poem is reborn from the ashes,
fluttering its wings.

夜思

月亮躲进了云层里，
房间内留着恰到好处的昏黄灯光。
我苦闷地坐在我的四十七公斤里，
烦恼占据重量的百分之三十。
我哪儿也去不了——
邻居把投诉的便条贴在大门上：
"麻烦晚上的音乐声音小一些"
试图封印住一只在盒子内蹦迪的怪兽……
怪我咯？怪我咯？
在这廉价出租房内的寡居青年
能不能埋怨你？
多少次夜深人静时把充电器摁在墙上，
发出的声音和重金属音乐大同小异。
我苦闷地坐在我的四十七公斤里，
烦恼占据重量的百分之三十。
我哪儿也不去了——
正版寡居青年不打算走出大门，
同二亿多高仿寡居青年混迹在一起。
月亮从云层后探出脑袋，
没见着新鲜事又躲进了云层里。

Deep at Night

The moon sat hidden in the clouds.
The dim glow in my room was just right.
At forty-seven kilograms, I sat there depressed,
with thirty percent of that weight taken up by worry.
There was nowhere else to go.

The neighbor hung a note on the door:
"*Please turn the music down*",
She tried to seal a beast dancing wildly in its bottle.
Blame me, huh?
As a young widow living in this cheap tenement,
did I ever blame you?
How many times have you plugged in that charger late at night?
Its sound was like heavy metal music to my ears.

At forty-seven kilograms, I sat there depressed.
with thirty percent of that weight taken up by worry.
There was nowhere else to go.

This young widow has no intention of walking out the door
to join more than 200 million other so-called singles.

The moon now poked its head out from behind the clouds.
And seeing nothing new in sight, it hid again.

月亮再次升起

月光皎洁,为远处的屋顶镀上一层银。
我四处张望,月色下不见心上人的身影。
不管你在哪里,请你抬起头,看月亮再次升起。
若是你在一艘来看我的慢船上,
那就起身离开拥挤的船舱来到开阔的甲板;
若是你在一架来看我的喷气飞机上,
那就取下结实的头盔观察你翱翔的天际。
黄昏将一捧星子倾撒进黑夜的口袋,
只是再次升起的月亮,
过于耀眼,黯淡了繁星。
我们站在同一片月色下,你看到的是月神的左脸颊,
我看到的是月神的右脸颊……
当我轻抚她的脸颊,
你变得触手可及。

The Moon Rises Again

The moon shines ever so bright,
basking the distant rooftop with hues of silver.
I looked around, without seeing my beloved under the moonlight.

Wherever you may be, my love —
look up to the sky and gaze upon the moon rising again.

If you're in a slow boat on your way to me,
stand up, leave the crowded cabin, and go out to the open deck.
If you're in a jet plane to see me,
take off your sturdy helmet
and watch the sky you're hovering over.

Twilight has scattered a handful of stars in the pockets of night.
But the rising moon is so bright that it obscures these stars.
You and I are under the same moonlight.
The left cheek of the moon goddess is before your eyes,
while her right cheek shines upon mine.
And whenever I reach out my hand to touch her,
you're suddenly within my reach again.

碎片

镜子变矮看不见脸了；
白墙需要重新粉刷了。

小镇上的年轻人都离开了，
雪花似的请柬飞舞着……
节假日他们默契地回到故乡举办一场婚礼，
他们的孩子大多选在 11 月出生。

"人是会变的。"
在人没有改变前，
这句话如同耳畔的微风吹过。
人因何而变？
某个瞬间，人意识到自己的变化：
是冰融化成水的过程，不易察觉……
静悄悄……

只有母亲没有变，
她还留在那个老房子里。
我不记得——
我们曾经那么亲密，那是我作为她的一部分。
今天我们一遍遍讨论食物，当地的天气。
在时间鸿沟之间的唯一桥梁上，
我遥望她
窗前的影子。

我该如何生活？当我知道
生活是场马拉松比赛，
所有人都奔向同一个终点。
又或者，生活是一条湍急的河流，
有人逆流而上，有人随波逐流——
还有人在河边悠闲垂钓。

Fragments

I've outgrown the mirror; my face is out of frame.
The white wall needs repainting.

All the young people in town have left.
Eventually, invitation cards will stream in like snowflakes,
as they silently return on holidays for their wedding ceremonies.
Most of their children will be born in November.

Many say: "*people change,*"
and before they even do,
these words of wisdom often fall on deaf ears.
But why do they change?
Only at a certain time do people notice these changes.
For it is like ice melting into water — silent and barely noticeable.

Mother is the only one who has not changed.
She still lives in that old house.
Let me remember how it was…
we used to be so close.
It was as if I grew up being a part of her.
Today we only talk about the food and the local weather,
over and over —
stranded on the only bridge across the abyss of time,
From a distance, I caught sight of her —
a silhouette looking out the window.

How then am I to live life
when I have realized that it is but a marathon?
Everyone is racing to the same end.
Life is otherwise a turbulent river,
where some go upstream, while others swim with the current.
Yet others fish the river in leisure.

梦魇

在固定的时间点，白日梦乍然结束，
绕过在秋风面前溃不成军的枯枝落叶，
那些街边闪烁着的路灯，是它们——
　　护送我回到温暖的房间。
我往绿豆上浇水，它们再也没能长出嫩芽。
我还能期待什么？阴雨连绵的日子
　　总不会有客人来访，
　　在这些伸手不见五指的夜晚，
　　狂风骤雨猛烈拍打过我的窗户。
彷徨，孤寂，悄无声息在地板上游走：
　　一条毒蛇滑进我的薄被。
当我将缠绕的藤蔓解开，窗外——
　　白雪已经坠落在群山之间。

Nightmare

At a certain point, the daydream suddenly ceases.
I walk past the dead branches and withered leaves
swirled by the autumn wind.

The streetlights flickering occasionally on both sides of the street
accompany me back to the warmth of my room.
I have watered the mung beans,
but new sprouts refuse to grow.

Oh, what did I expect?

On rainy days,
no one ever comes to visit.
On those dark nights,
rainstorms knock violently on my window.
Perplexity and loneliness seep in, creeping across the floor,
and like a poisonous snake, it slithers into my thin sheets.
And when I sort this tangled vine,
outside the window,
snow has fallen between the mountains and is melting.

给我带一枝玫瑰来吧…

亲爱的,给我带一枝玫瑰来吧。
我只请求一次,膝盖微微弯曲——
　　(你仔细观察,会发现)
是的,我永远只会卑微一次——
　　依靠哀求,获得的礼物
　　失去了令人愉悦的价值。
我只想要玫瑰,爱神鲜血灌溉过——
　　白玫瑰花丛中的任意一朵。
待到心灰意冷之时,你才将红蔷薇奉上,
　　又怎能怪我弃之如履?

Bring me a Rose

Darling, bring me a rose.
I shall ask only once on slightly bended knees.
(If you have sharp eyes, you will surely not miss it).

Yes, I will humble myself just once.
Gifts that were begged for
never once delighted my heart.

What I ask from you is a solitary rose,
any one from the white rose bushes,
irrigated by Aphrodite herself.

But if I grow weary of waiting...
give me a wild red rose in its stead —
but don't blame me if I toss it away.

关系

我不轻易说爱，别看爱——
只有一个字。一旦被你听见，
你就会为此谱曲，三个音符，
值得反复弹奏？我...昏昏欲睡。

我说，它是一种关系，
形容事物之间，在同一个空间的
所有状态。静物素描中
把香蕉画在苹果的左边，
它是一种预告，乌云密布，酝酿，
迟迟不见雨水落下。

答应我，不轻易对我说爱，别看爱——
只有一个字。一旦你说出口，
两只自由鸟就被关进一个笼子里。

唉，我去你的精神家园旅行过——
那里一片荒芜。你的青春，你的靓丽
是海市蜃楼。我的确为这幻境震撼，
只是风吹云动，终究不会久留。

我最好保持沉默，你也什么都别说！

The Relationship

I do not speak of love so casually,
even if it is but a mere word.
At the slight mention of it,
it is worthy of composing a beautiful melody.
With three notes, it is worth playing over and over to me
until I surrender to sleep.

The way I put it, it is a relationship
that describes the state of things in the same space.
Just like in a sketch of a still moment in life,
the banana is always depicted on the left side of the apple.
It is like a forecast with dark clouds on the horizon,
and a thunderstorm will soon emerge.
But an imminent downpour is nowhere in sight.

So, promise me,
do not speak of love to me so casually,
even if it is but a mere word.
As soon as it rolls off your tongue,
two free birds are locked in a cage.

Alas! I traveled to your spiritual home,
finding that it is a barren land.
Your sweet youth and beauty,
like a mirage, they tantalized me.
But the wind will blow, and the clouds will scatter,
they will not linger for long.

So, I might as well keep silent.
And you're better off saying nothing at all.

海子和我的祖国

祖国，一头雄狮沉睡
在东方——
红日冉冉升起，
万丈光芒——

五千年来……
烽火烧着，星在天空中烧着，
烧出83个王朝，
华夏文明不灭的火光，
烧出一个深刻的烙印 —— 中华
我携带它，在母亲古老的身体里孕育——
大江大河在我的血管里流淌。

黄河咆哮，奔腾入海——
犹闻城墙下妇女哭泣，寸断肝肠；
长江水啊，长江水啊——
一张密网撒下去，没有躲开的银鱼都是口粮。

我的祖国，
也是海子的祖国。
我们有幸生于祖国的河岸边，
以梦为马的诗人们何去何从——
太阳比长安离海子更近。

我以梦为马驰骋，看
西方残阳映照千秋雪，
北冥有鱼来踏南海浪。
我以梦为马——
抵达太阳之前，
我在月亮的驿站暂歇，
备好干草，清水——
马儿今夜在马厩入睡。

An Ode to the Motherland

The motherland is like a sleeping lion in the East.
Behold, the red sun rises,
shining in all its splendor.

For five thousand years,
the beacon of fire has been burning bright,
the stars blaze in the sky,
eighty-three imperial dynasties arose, one after another.
The inextinguishable flame of civilization
has burned a deep imprint in our hearts — China.
With it, I was conceived in the ancient body of our motherland.
Great rivers flow in my veins.

The Yellow River roars and surges into the sea,
and its howls are reminiscent of the woman
sobbing at the foot of the Great Wall.
Along the Yangtze River, a fishing net is cast out,
and the whitebaits that had not escaped are fished for a living.

My motherland is also the motherland of Hai Zi,
a great poet of modern times.
How fortunate we are to be born on the banks of the great river.
Where did our great poets go —
the poets whose dreams mounted wild horses?
The sun is perhaps closer to Haizi than to Chang'an.

My dreams, too, are mounted on a wild horse running free.
The sunset in the west shines down upon the everlasting snow.
The fish of the North China Sea swims
in the mighty waves of the South China Sea.

My dreams and I are mounted on a wild horse.
And before I ride anew to reach the sun,
I lay to rest in the post station of the moon,
to prepare hay and clean water —
for tonight, my horse will rest in the stable.

存在的意义

世界如海纳百川,
一个人就是沧海一粟,
有时候一个人忍不住思考:
既然生老病死是每个人无法逃避的宿命,
那么人存在的意义是什么?

一个人陷入这个哲学味道颇浓的问题,
无法自拔,
许多人心里有可能也思考过这个问题,
尽管一些人看上去只关心衣食住行。

世界史海钩沉,由很多人书写。
一个人就是一本史书,
有波澜壮阔也有宁静淡泊,
有精彩绝伦也有索然无味,
后来人总能找到感兴趣的故事。

The Meaning of Existence

The world is like an ocean that flows into millions of rivers.
A man is but a drop in that water.
Sometimes, one can't help but think:
Since the course of birth,
aging, disease, and death will always be our inescapable fate.
Tell me, what is then the meaning of our existence?

A man who finds himself lost in this philosophical question
will never find his way out.
This may have gone through the minds of many people,
even if some only care about their daily needs.

History has given birth to numerous great individuals
but it needs the next generation
to further engage in the search for the profound truth.
For a man is a history book himself,
written with texts of wild torrents and calm waters,
delightful moments and dreary years.
And later generations who search for this evasive truth
will always find endless stories, both interesting and compelling.

萨福套娃

千年之前的某个夜晚——
　月亮掉下来——
　　萨福独卧
写了一首小诗。

　　今夜
　　我独卧。
月亮掉下来——
　读着萨福的诗歌
　写了一首短诗：
多年以后的某个夜晚，
　　月落星沉，
　　月亮和星星，
你所见和我们所见不是同一批次。
　谁会读萨福的诗歌？
　她比我先成为一名诗人。
谁会独卧读完这首诗歌再去读萨福的诗歌？
　我比你先成为一名诗人。
谁会闲来无事写一首长诗记录读诗的时刻？
　谁会先成为一名诗人？

The Russian Dolls of Sappho

One night, a thousand years ago,
as the moon was setting on the horizon,
Sappho wrote a modest poem
as she lay alone.

Tonight,
the moon sets as it did back then,
as I, too, lie alone,
reading Sappho's poems,
I also began to write a modest poem.
And one night, many lifetimes later,
the delicate moon and the stars will also set.
The moon and the stars that you will see then
will not be the ones we see now.

Who will eventually read the poems of Sappho?
She became a poet long before I did.
Who will be the next to lie alone,
and read this poem before moving on to Sappho's poems?
I became a poet long before you did,
for the one who spends time writing a long poem
to capture the moment of reading a poem
would be the poet first.

灵魂

我们是同一根树干分岔长出的树枝,朝向九个鎏金太阳的方向;
我们是同一个鸟巢相拥而眠的雏鸟,奥,拥抱是张开的柔软银色羽翼。

我们对万事万物有相同的感受,
我现在的感受是你现在的感受。
为何如此?
我们的灵魂必定相识已久——
不然我该如何解释只言片语间,
一股难以言述的熟悉感就涌上心头。

我们是同一株蒲公英身上掉下来的种子,
乘着风的飞天魔毯撒到了不同的角落。
相隔千山万水,即便如此——
我现在的感受应该是你现在的感受——
从坚硬的石缝中破土而出!
沉重,阴冷,企图撕裂隔绝光的那道屏障!
破茧而出,控诉所经历的阵痛。
你根本不该为我敲响时间如白驹过隙的警钟,
快乐只属于愚昧永远装睡的人!
那时我的意识在黑暗中,沉迷于美妙的催眠曲不愿醒来,
靡靡之音,终日虚度,多么幸福!

Souls

We are branches of the same tree trunk, forking out,
gazing in the direction of the nine golden suns.
We are nestlings huddled together in the same nest,
with soft silver wings spread out.

We have the same feelings about all things.
How I feel now is how you also feel.
How is that so?
Because our souls must have known each other long before.
How else could I concisely explain
the subtle feeling of familiarity that overwhelms my heart?

We are the seeds that fell from the same dandelion,
scattered to various corners on the flying magic carpet of the wind.
Though thousands of mountains and rivers keep us apart,
how I feel now should also be how you feel.
We are the seeds breaking out of the earth between hard rocks,
and braving the frigid cold and cramped space,
struggling to break through the barrier
that cuts us off from the light.
Breaking out of the earth,
we begin to denounce the spasms of pain we have endured.

Time flies, I know, but you shouldn't have set off the alarm clock.
Happiness belongs only to the fools who pretend to be asleep.
For at that time, my consciousness lurked in the dark.
I fell asleep to a beautiful lullaby and did not desire to be awakened.
For at that time, I was helplessly entranced by its paralyzing melody
and spent the day lost in its music.
Oh, how blissful it was!

窗后的猫

我看见有东西在那边——
有趣的,
兴奋的,
诱人的,
我希望我可以触碰它们,与它们玩耍,
成为它们的一部分,
仿佛它们由物质构成。
然后我猜想,它们真的存在吗?
但是,不管它们是属于我的过去、现在还是未来,
不管它们是回忆,现实还是希望,
不管它们是否只是我想象的结果
…这都不重要
玻璃将它们与我隔绝开来。
我认为我从很久以前,
就一直在注视着它们。

The Cat Behind the Window

I see something out there —
Interesting.
Exciting.
Inviting.
How I wish I could touch them,
play with them,
and be a part of them
as if they were made of matter.

I wonder if they are really there.
But whether they belong to my past, present, or future,
whether they are memories, realities, or hopes,
or merely products of my imagination,
it doesn't really matter.
The glass will just keep us apart.
And I have been watching them for a long time now.

风铃

我通过风铃听到风声,
我从树下的阴影中想象太阳,
我将视线延展至沙漠中的花朵去触摸雨水,
我知道你存在是因为我内心的回声,
我知道我爱你是因为我内心的空虚。

Wind Chimes

I hear the breeze through the wind chimes.
I imagine how the sun looks like through the shadows under a tree.
I feel the rain by stretching my eyes
over the blooming flowers of the desert.
I know that you are out there
because your echo resounds in my heart.
So, I know that I love you and long for you
for there is a hollow inside of my soul.

夜回声

如果我是那位邻居,
我会珍惜你的吉他弦,绝无埋怨;
如果我是风,
我会把音符带到遥远的未知之地;
如果我是夜晚,
我会让蟋蟀安静下来不打扰小夜曲;
而如果我是白昼,
我会迫不及待夜晚归来。

The Echoes of Melody at Night

If I were your neighbor,
I would relish the melody humming from the strings of your guitar.
Not once shall I ever complain.
If I were the wind,
I would carry your notes to distant lands unknown.
If I were the night,
I would silence the chirping crickets
should they ever disrupt your sweet serenade.
And if I were the day,
I would hastily give way to the night.

www.ingramcontent.com/pod-product-compliance
Lightning Source LLC
Chambersburg PA
CBHW070439010526
44118CB00014B/2112